W9-BSB-866

SCIENCE IN THE REAL WORLD

States of Matter in the Real World

by Roberta Baxter

Content Consultant
Dr. Tony Borgerding
Professor of Chemistry
University of St. Thomas

Published by ABDO Publishing Company, PO Box 398166, Minneapolis, MN 55439.

Printed in the United States of America,
North Mankato, Minnesota
112012
012013
THIS BOOK CONTAINS AT LEAST 10% RECYCLED MATERIALS.

Editor: Karen Latchana Kenney
Series Designer: Becky Daum

Cataloging-in-Publication Data
Baxter, Roberta.
States of matter in the real world / Roberta Baxter.
p. cm. -- (Science in the real world)
Includes bibliographical references and index.
ISBN 978-1-61783-745-6
1. Matter--Juvenile literature. 2. Matter--Constitution--Juvenile literature. 3. Matter--Properties--Juvenile literature. I. Title.
530.4--dc21

2012946823

Photo Credits: Boris Franz/Shutterstock Images, cover, 1; Babek Tafreshi/SSPL/Getty Images, 4; Shutterstock Images, 7, 19, 20, 22, 26, 32, 35; Mansell/Time Life Pictures/Getty Images, 8; Hulton Archive/Getty Images, 11; Rainer Plendl/Shutterstock Images, 14; Carlos Caetano/Shutterstock Images, 16; Stanislav Sokolov/Shutterstock Images, 25; Red Line Editorial, 28; Vlad Ghiea/Shutterstock Images, 29, 45; Andreas Solaro/AFP/Getty Images, 37; Rune Stoltz Bertinussen/AFP/Getty Images, 38

CONTENTS

CHAPTER ONE

What Are States of Matter?

The world around us is made of matter. Matter is made of tiny particles that we can't see, called atoms. They take up space and have mass. The chair you sit on, the air around you, your body, and even the stars are made of matter.

Matter comes in different forms. Water is an example. It is a liquid you drink or see in an ocean. But water also exists as solid ice and as gaseous steam

The stars of the Milky Way galaxy, as seen above Brazil, are made of matter.

from a teapot. Steam, liquid water, and ice are the states of matter of water.

All matter can exist in these three states. Some substances will be liquids at room temperature, while others will be solids or gases. It depends on the substance. The state of matter of any substance can be changed. A fourth state of matter, called plasma, can be found in stars and lightning.

Changing States

The state of matter of any substance can be changed. A solid changes to a liquid if heat is added. A liquid becomes a gas if heated. A gas changes to liquid when it cools. Liquids also change to solids in lower temperatures.

Everyday Matter

The electricity in your home may come from a power plant that heats water until it turns to steam. The steam turns a big machine that produces the electricity. Air conditioners and refrigerators work by making liquid change to gas and back again.

Water turns to gas when heated in a teapot.

CHAPTER TWO

Early Studies of Matter

Ancient Greek philosophers Democritus and Leucippus thought about the nature of matter. They guessed that it was possible to cut matter into its smallest pieces. They called those pieces *atomos* (or atoms). They also believed that atoms could not be destroyed. And they thought that atoms were combined in different ways to make all the things on Earth. Their idea of atoms was different from what

Greek philosopher Democritus thought about what matter was made from on Earth.

current scientists know about atoms. But the ancient Greeks had a great start to understanding matter.

Early Experiments

Early scientists knew of solids and liquids. They combined the two in different ways. Some noticed chemical reactions between the two that caused bubbles. Scientists later discovered that these bubbles were another form of matter—gas.

Scientist Robert Boyle investigated air. In 1660 he found that it could be compressed. His work resulted in Boyle's law. This law was about how the volume of gas related to pressure.

In 1756 Joseph Black found a gas that would not allow a candle to

Squeezed Air

Scientist Robert Boyle built a J-shaped glass tube. His assistant poured mercury, a heavy liquid, into the top of the tube. The mercury trapped a pocket of air in the short end. Boyle measured the air pocket. When more mercury was poured in, the pocket shrank. The air was squeezed together. This meant the air could be compressed.

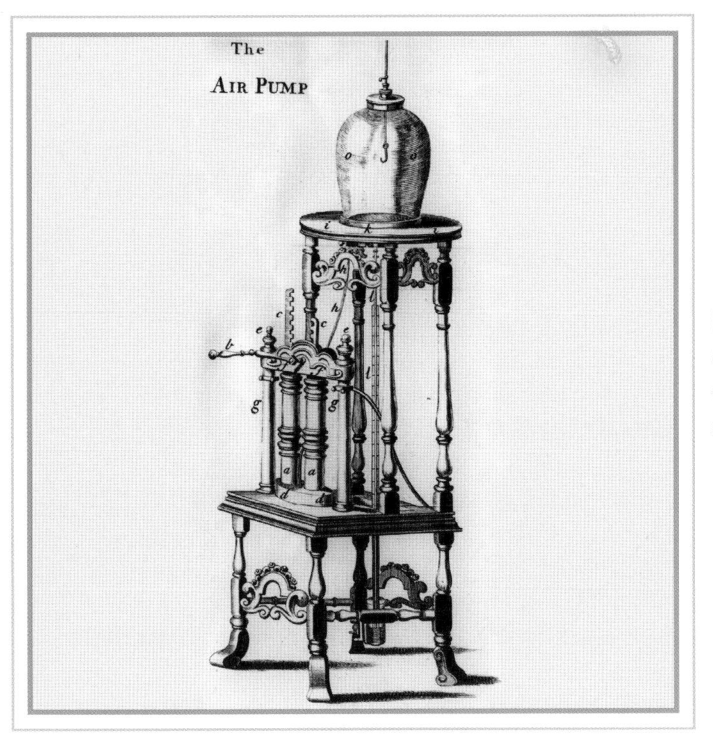

Robert Boyle used an air pump for his experiments with air and pressure.

burn. He called it "fixed air," but we now know it as carbon dioxide. Ten years later Henry Cavendish announced the discovery of the gas we call hydrogen. In 1774 Joseph Priestley produced a gas that would make a candle burn more brightly. He breathed in some of the gas. He said it made him breathe light and easy. He had discovered oxygen.

From 1772 to 1777, chemist Antoine Lavoisier discovered that air was made of more than one gas. Lavoisier also studied chemical reactions. He found that matter never disappears. It only changes form. This was the basis for the law of the conservation of mass. This theory states that in chemical reactions, mass is neither created nor destroyed.

Studying Atoms

In 1897 English scientist J. J. Thompson discovered the electron. People at the time knew that atoms were in all matter, but they did not know that atoms were made of smaller parts. Atoms are too small to see, so not much was known about them. Also around this time, scientist Marie Curie studied substances, such as uranium, that let off rays of energy. Ernest Rutherford showed that an atom's nucleus was small and dense in 1911. Then in 1913 Niels Bohr came up with the atomic model. This model showed that electrons moved in rings around the nucleus of an atom. He said that electrons could jump from one ring to another.

By learning more about atoms, these and other scientists discovered more about the nature of matter.

STRAIGHT TO THE SOURCE

Author Jim Baggot wrote in his book *The Quantum Story* about important moments in the study of the atom. Baggot included a quote from Niels Bohr discussing his atomic model:

> *"These models," [Bohr] had said, "have been deduced, or if you prefer, guessed, from experiments, not [proven math equations]. I hope that they describe the structure of atoms as well, but only as well, as is possible in the descriptive language of classical physics. We must be clear that, when it comes to atoms, language can be used only as in poetry. The poet, too, is not nearly so concerned with describing facts as with creating images and establishing mental connections."*
>
> *Source: Jim Baggot.* The Quantum Story: A History in 40 Moments. *New York: Oxford University Press, 2011. Print. 47.*

Consider Your Audience

Read this passage closely. How could you adapt Bohr's words for a modern audience, such as your neighbors or your classmates? Write a blog post giving this same information to the new audience. What is the most effective way to get your point across to this audience? How is the language you use for the new audience different from Bohr's original text? Why?

CHAPTER THREE

Solids Hold Their Shape

Much of the world is made up of solid materials. Wood, metal, and paper are all solids. We even use the word *solid* to mean something that is firm and strong.

What Is a Solid?

The atoms in matter have energy. They vibrate at different speeds. The amount of energy in matter determines if something is liquid, gas, or solid. Lots

Car frames are made from metal, which is a solid.

In solids, atoms are packed together but also have some space between them, similar to the balls in this picture.

of energy leads to a gas. Less energy leads to a solid state of matter.

Atoms are packed closely together in solids. Imagine some balls packed in a box. There is space between the balls, but not very much. Each ball touches several others. Like balls in a box, atoms in the solid state cannot be compressed.

Volume and Shape

Volume is how much space something takes up. If the same number of balls is put in a deeper box, the volume of the balls will stay the same. If you put salt in a test tube, it might take up half the tube. If it is spread out over the table, it looks different but still has the same volume. Atoms also keep the same volume. A solid will hold its shape unless a physical force acts on it. For example, a wad of clay will hold its shape unless someone starts squeezing it into a different shape.

Atoms in a solid state vibrate slowly because they have only a small amount of energy. They are attracted to one another so they stick together. When heat is added, the atoms vibrate faster. This can make a solid change its state. It can turn into a liquid.

Crystals

Many solids have a crystal structure. That means they have a regular, repeating pattern. Table salt and sugar may appear the same, but if you look at both

Studying Crystals

In the 1940s and 1950s, Dorothy Crowfoot Hodgkin studied crystals to figure out the three-dimensional structures of some really big molecules. She used X-rays on crystals to learn about the molecules' structures. Through her studies, Hodgkin discovered the structure of penicillin, an antibiotic, and insulin, a chemical that helps our bodies use sugar for energy. Hodgkin was awarded the 1964 Nobel Prize in Chemistry for her work.

under a microscope you will see a difference. The crystals of salt are cubic, like building blocks. Sugar crystals are longer and have six sides, like a hexagon. Another crystal is snow. Water droplets freeze into six-sided snowflakes with many different side branches and arms.

We can see the unique crystal structures of snowflakes when they are magnified.

CHAPTER FOUR

Flowing Liquids

Another state of matter is liquid. Water is the most common liquid found on Earth. Many liquids, such as milk, juice, and soft drinks, are mostly water. But other liquids include alcohols and gasoline.

Same Volume, Different Shapes

Atoms in liquids move past one another. They still pull toward each other, but they are not packed as tightly

Water is found in lakes, rivers, and oceans on Earth.

Liquids take on the shapes of their containers.

together as the atoms in solids. Most liquids, except for water, do not form crystals as solids do.

In one way liquids are like solids. They keep the same volume regardless of what container they are in. An amount of milk might look like more in a tall, skinny glass than in a short, fat one. But if the amounts were measured, they would be the same. The milk took on the shape of the glass but had the same volume.

Liquids are also very different from solids. Liquids take the shape of whatever container they are in.

They don't keep their shape as solids do. Instead they spread out to fill the container. Liquids can't be compressed or squeezed closer together. The atoms are already close to one another.

Atoms in liquids have more energy than those in solids and less than those in gases. Atoms in liquids slide past other atoms. This makes liquids flow. Liquids change state when heated or cooled. Adding heat turns a liquid into a gas. Cooling a liquid changes it into a solid.

Surface Tension

One way liquids are different from the other states of matter is that they have surface tension. Think of water hitting a newly waxed car. The water forms beads on the car rather than flowing

Water Is Different

Most solids are denser than the liquid state of the same substance. The solid will sink to the bottom of a container holding the liquid. Water is different. Ice is the solid form of water. And ice is less dense than liquid water. Ice does not sink. It floats. This is important to fish in a lake. During winter some of the water freezes above and protects the fish below.

over it. This happens because of surface tension. The molecules of water are more strongly attached to one another than they are to the wax on the car. This causes beads to form. Surface tension also allows some insects, such as a water strider, to walk on water.

FURTHER EVIDENCE

There was quite a bit of information about liquids in Chapter Four. It covered the properties of liquids, including surface tension. But if you could pick out the main point of the chapter, what would it be? What evidence was given to support that point? Visit the Web site below to learn more about surface tension and water. Choose a quote from the Web site that relates to this chapter. Does this quote support the author's main point? Does it make a new point? Write a few sentences explaining how the quote you found relates to this chapter.

What Is Surface Tension?

www.epa.gov/owow/NPS/kids/surfacetension.html

Water striders use surface tension to walk on water.

CHAPTER FIVE

Moving Gases

The third common state of matter is gas. Air is a mixture of gases. The reaction when baking soda and vinegar are mixed results in a bubbling gas. This is carbon dioxide. You can also see this gas as bubbles in a soft drink or sparkling water.

Volume and Shape

Gases take the shape of whatever container they are placed in. They have no shape of their own.

The bubbles in sparkling water are caused by a gas in the water.

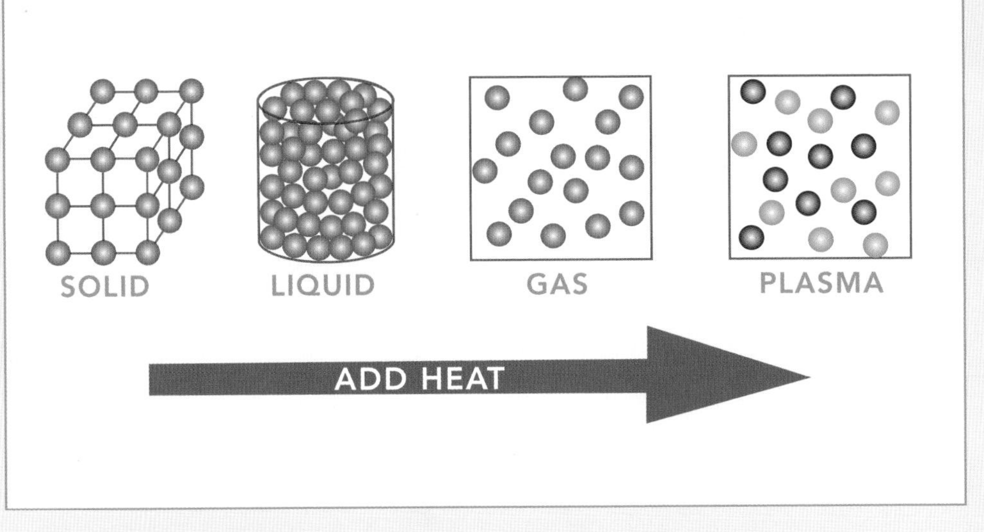

Moving Atoms

The atoms in different states of matter move at different speeds. They also have more or less space between them. Take a look at this diagram. Compare how the information is conveyed visually in the diagram with how it's conveyed in the text. How are they similar? How are they different?

If an amount of gas in a small container is let into a larger container, the gas will fill up the larger container.

In solids and liquids, atoms are strongly attracted to one another. But in gases, there is only a weak attraction. Each gas atom bounces in every direction. It does not slow down and stop. This state of matter has much more energy than either liquids or solids.

Gases fill up and take the shape of hot air balloons.

Gases exert pressure. The pressure comes from the gas atoms hitting the sides of the container. Gases can be compressed into smaller places. If a force is applied to compress the gas, the atoms squeeze together. For example air inside a partly filled balloon can be compressed into a tight section of the balloon.

Compressed Gas

A bottle of liquid oxygen can hold a large amount of gaseous oxygen. The bottle of gaseous oxygen can be easily strapped to a person's back or rolled on a little cart. Compression makes it easy to carry around a large amount of a gas in a small container.

Changing State

When a gas cools, the atoms slow down. They stick to each other. They turn into a liquid. The ability to compress gases by squeezing them with pressure is very useful. Scuba divers and people needing oxygen because of health problems use tanks of compressed oxygen. Inside the tanks the oxygen is a liquid. It expands when it is released. It turns back into a gas to be breathed. Another property of gas is its ability to diffuse. Perfumes and even the scent of a skunk turn quickly from a liquid into a gas. Then the gas mixes with the air, spreading the smell.

STRAIGHT TO THE SOURCE

Antoine Lavoisier studied gases in the 1700s. He wrote about the nature of gases in *Memoir on the Combustion in General*:

> *All bodies in nature present themselves to us in three different states. Some are solid like stones, earth, salt, and metals. Others are fluid like water, mercury, spirits of wine; and others finally are in a third state which I shall call the state of expansion or of vapours. . . The same body can pass successfully through each of these states, and in order to make this phenomenon occur it is necessary only to combine it with a greater or lesser quantity of the matter of fire.*
>
> *Source: William H. Brock.* The Norton History of Chemistry. *New York: W. W. Norton & Co., 1992. Print. 98.*

What's the Big Idea?

Take a close look at Lavoisier's words. What is his main idea? What evidence does he use to support this idea? Come up with a few sentences showing how Lavoisier uses two or three pieces of evidence to support his main point.

CHAPTER SIX

Changing States of Matter

Changing from one state to another involves energy, usually in the form of heat. The heat can be added or removed.

For a solid to melt into a liquid, the attractions between its atoms must be weakened. When heat is added, atoms gain enough energy to partially overcome the attractions rigidly holding them

Metal turns to liquid if it is heated to a high temperature.

Refrigerators: Liquid to Gas

In a refrigerator, a machine squeezes a gas. The gas condenses into a liquid. It flows through a coil and then quickly expands into a gas. Changing from a liquid to a gas takes energy, and everything nearby becomes colder.

together in a solid. The solid becomes a liquid by melting.

The same happens when a liquid turns into a gas. The atoms gain energy from heat and completely overcome the attractions holding them together. The atoms begin moving around very fast and in a random manner. This makes the liquid turn into a gas. This process is called vaporization. When a liquid boils and evaporates, it is part of this process.

Taking Away Heat

When heat is taken away, the states of matter also change. Cooling a gas will turn it into a liquid. This process is called condensation. A liquid freezes into a solid when heat is taken away. Compression can also turn gases into liquids.

Dry ice turns from solid to gas without a liquid state in between.

Some substances can change from a solid to a gas without the liquid stage. This is called sublimation. Sometimes snow will disappear when the solid crystal turns into water vapor. Solid carbon dioxide, or dry ice, also turns from a solid to a gas.

Deposition is the opposite of sublimation. Deposition is occurring when frost builds up on a window.

Identifying Substances

Melting temperature and boiling point can be used to identify unknown substances. A melting temperature is the point at which a solid substance melts. The

Chemical name	Melting point	Boiling point
Gold	1945.4°F (1063°C)	
Yellow brass	1661°F to 1709.6°F (905°C to 932°C)	
Methanol (Wood Alcohol)		148.93°F (64.96°C)
Isopropanol (Rubbing Alcohol)		180.5°F (82.5°C)
Water	32°F (0°C)	212°F (100°C)

Melting and Boiling Points

Here are some melting and boiling points that can be used to identify chemicals. Take a look at this chart. What do these temperatures tell you about the chemicals in the table? How might a scientist use this information?

boiling point of a liquid is the temperature at which it turns into a gas. Suppose you had two gold-colored pieces of metal and you needed to find out which one is gold. If you melted one and it turned into a liquid at 1945.4 degrees Fahrenheit (1063°C), then that piece is gold. If the piece melted at a lower temperature, then it is not gold. It is yellow brass. Two types of chemicals called alcohols are both clear liquids. But their boiling temperatures are different. This identifies the liquids.

A metal worker melts gold at a very high and specific temperature.

CHAPTER SEVEN

Plasma In the Stars

Another state of matter is seen in the stars. It is called plasma. Because plasma exists in the stars, it is the most common state of matter in the universe. This state of matter has a changing volume and shape. In gases the atoms zoom around with their electrons intact. But in plasma the electrons are stripped away from the atom by an enormous amount of energy.

A green aurora borealis display, made from plasma particles reacting with Earth's atmosphere, glows over a city in Norway.

Aurora Borealis

These natural colorful light shows happen 60 to 620 miles (96 to 997 km) above Earth. Most have a green color. Displays that are very high in the atmosphere have a red or purple color.

Sir William Crookes described the plasma state of matter in 1879. American chemist Dr. Irving Langmuir gave plasma its name in 1923. A gas can become plasma when heated to extremely high temperatures, such as those found in our sun and other stars. The sun releases plasma plumes from its surface. These plasma particles travel to Earth. This flow is called the solar wind. When it reaches Earth, the energy of the plasma hits gas atoms in the atmosphere and causes them to glow. The result is the aurora borealis (the northern lights) or the aurora australis (the southern lights). Plasma also occurs in lightning.

On Earth scientists have learned to make the plasma state and to control it. Some televisions and all fluorescent lights contain plasma. The plasma they contain is created from electric currents sent through gas.

The states of matter are an important part of our world. Everything we see and touch is a solid, liquid, gas, or plasma. The next time you feel a popsicle melting in your mouth, see a lightning bolt, or touch a table, you will be experiencing the different states of matter.

EXPLORE ONLINE

The focus in Chapter Seven was plasma. It also touched upon where plasma is found. The Web site below focuses on the same subjects. As you know, every source is different. How is the information given in the Web site different from the information in this chapter? What information is the same? How do the two sources present information differently? What can you learn from this Web site?

Plasma Basics

www.chem4kids.com/files/matter_plasma.html

IMPORTANT DATES

1660
Robert Boyle shows that air can be compressed.

1756
Joseph Black discovers carbon dioxide.

1766
Henry Cavendish discovers hydrogen.

1774
Joseph Priestley discovers oxygen.

1879
Sir William Crookes discovers plasma.

1897
J. J. Thompson discovers the electron.

1911
Ernest Rutherford describes an atom's nucleus as small and dense.

1913
Niels Bohr creates an atomic model.

1923
Irving Langmuir names the new state of matter plasma.

1940s–1950s
Dorothy Crowfoot Hodgkin studies crystals to understand the structure of large molecules.

OTHER WAYS YOU CAN FIND STATES OF MATTER IN THE REAL WORLD

Helium Balloons

Helium balloons float high in the sky. Helium is a gas that is less dense than air. Since helium is lighter, it floats in air. But a helium balloon in the air will soon be down on the ground. Why? Helium is a very small atom, and it leaks out of the balloon. It diffuses through the wall of the balloon, so the balloon does not float anymore.

What Is the Dew Point?

The dew point is a measure of how much water vapor is in the air. You might hear the dew point mentioned on a weather forecast. If the temperature cools to the dew point, the water vapor condenses out of the air and becomes dew or fog. The dew point is always lower than or equal to the air temperature.

Melting Ice

In winter you might spread solid salt on an icy sidewalk. The salt makes the ice melt, turning that solid into a liquid. One solid changes the state of another solid.

Say What?

Studying about the states of matter can mean learning a lot of new vocabulary. Find five words in this book you've never seen or heard before. Use a dictionary to find out what they mean. Then write the meanings in your own words, and use each word in a new sentence.

Another View

There are many sources online and in your library about the states of matter. Ask a librarian or other adult to help you find a reliable source on states of matter. Compare what you learn in this new source and what you have found out in this book. Then write a short essay comparing and contrasting the new source's view of states of matter to the ideas in this book. How are they different? How are they similar? Why do you think they are different or similar?

You Are There

Imagine that you are in Antoine Lavoisier's laboratory trying to discover what gases are in air. How would you measure the different gases, and what equipment would you need? What would your results be? What challenges would you have in doing the research?

Surprise Me

Learning about states of matter can be interesting and surprising. What two or three facts about states of matter did you find most surprising? Write a few sentences about each fact. Why did you find them surprising?

GLOSSARY

atoms
tiny particles that make up matter

compressed
squeezed together

condensation
turning a gas into a liquid

crystal
a solid with a regular repeating pattern

dense
heavy

deposition
the action of matter being deposited in a layer on something

diffuse
spread out

energy
the ability to do work

molecule
combination of atoms bound together

sublimation
going from a solid directly to a gas

vaporization
changing into a vapor or gas

volume
the amount of space taken up by matter

LEARN MORE

Books

Brent, Lynnette. *States of Matter.* New York: Crabtree Publishing Company, 2008.

Johnson, Rebecca L. *Atomic Structure*. Minneapolis, MN: Twenty-First Century Books, 2008.

Peppas, Lynn. *What Is a Gas?* New York: Crabtree Publishing Company, 2013.

Web Links

To learn more about states of matter, visit ABDO Publishing Company online at **www.abdopublishing.com**. Web sites about states of matter are featured on our Book Links page. These links are routinely monitored and updated to provide the most current information available.

Visit **www.mycorelibrary.com** for free additional tools for teachers and students.

INDEX

ABOUT THE AUTHOR

Roberta Baxter has a degree in chemistry and enjoys writing about science for students of all ages. She also writes books about history and biographies, as well as articles on a wide range of subjects.